THE HALF-TIDY BOOK OF WELSH JOKES

This book is respectfully dedicated to the people of Cardiganshire – the Cardis – without whose tireless devotion to not spending a penny more than absolutely necessary, the world would be an unfunnier place.

If you have any Welsh jokes, particularly Cardi ones, you are welcome to send them to

huwjamescardiff@hotmail.com

Needless to say, no payments of any sort can be expected.

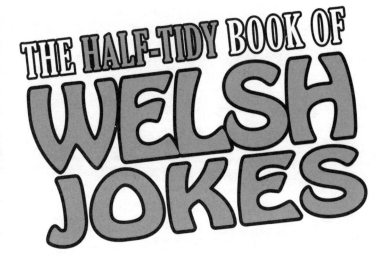

THE HALF-TIDY BOOK OF WELSH JOKES

Huw James

y Lolfa

First impression: 2010

© Huw James & Y Lolfa Cyf., 2010

Illustrations: Mark Morgan
Cover: Alan Thomas

ISBN: 9781847712059

Printed on acid-free and partly recycled paper
and published and bound in Wales by
Y Lolfa Cyf., Talybont, Ceredigion SY24 5HE
e-mail ylolfa@ylolfa.com
website www.ylolfa.com
tel 01970 832 304
fax 832 782

Contents

Mountain Rescue

Do you remember the Big Freeze of 1963? According to the Met Office it was the coldest winter since 1740 when the Thames froze. Large parts of Cardiganshire were covered in several feet of snow. Many animals were buried and the various Mountain Rescue teams were called out to look for them. My cousin Ianto led one of the teams.

What they did was to stretch out in a line – five of them – driving long poles into the snow as they went along. After a fairly short time, Ianto thought he had found something that was well above the level of the surrounding area. They all hurriedly used their spades to dig down about five feet and discovered, to their surprise, what appeared to be the chimney of a habitable dwelling. (Or what, if I wasn't a solicitor, I would probably call a house. But then, as my principal used to say when I was an articled clerk, "Why use one simple word when two complicated ones will do?")

Anyway, Ianto leant down to shout down the chimney: "Is anybody there?"

For some time there was no reply. Then up the chimney came the voice of someone with a thin, suspicious, Cardiganshire accent: "Who is it?"

Ianto leant down again: "It's the Mountain Rescue."

Another pause and then the same voice said, "We've already given."

The Death Bed

Uncle Jack worked to the end. In fact he was seventy-six years old when he collapsed while driving his tractor. Ianto got him back to the house and called the doctor. Uncle Jack had not recovered consciousness and the doctor told Aunty Megan to expect the worst.

So that night Aunty Megan and Ianto sat by the bedside waiting for the end. After an hour Jack seemed to stir and made sounds as if he was trying to say something. Megan leaned forward anxiously and said, "Yes, Jack, I am here. What is it?"

The old man struggled to get his words out. "Write this down," he said.

Megan grabbed a pencil and a piece of paper.

"Last Tuesday I went to the market in Lampeter. I sold a heifer to Tom Evans, Pant-y-Groes. He owes me £803.10," he managed to gasp out just before relapsing into unconsciousness.

Pride mingled with sadness on Megan's face as she looked across at Ianto and said, "You see – to the very end – mind as sharp as a needle."

Another hour passed before Jack started to stir again. At once Megan was ready with pen and paper. Jack's voice came again – barely audible this time: "Last Thursday I went to Tregaron Mart... Gwilym Thomas... a ewe... £248."

Megan quickly wrote it down, turning to her son as she finished. "Even in his last hours," she sighed, "as acute as ever."

Another hour passed before more stirring and sounds came from Jack – but they were different this

time. Megan and Ianto thought that this was surely the end. But not quite yet. One final instruction was to come: "Last Saturday… went to Cardigan… Idris Shoes… bought some Wellingtons… I owe him six pounds."

Megan allowed the pen and paper to drop into her lap.

"Well," she said resignedly, "beginning to ramble."

Welshman on a Desert Island

Dai is on board a ship which founders and he finds himself washed up on a desert island. He remains there for ten years until he manages to attract the attention of a passing ship. When the landing party arrives he proudly shows them around his island.

First he shows them his house which is made out of banana leaves. The visitors are duly impressed. But there are two other buildings made out of banana leaves – one with a spire, the other with a tower.

"What are those?" they ask.

"Churches," he replies.

"But why two churches?"

"Well," he explains, pointing to the one with

a tower, "that is the one I go to. The other," he says, pointing at the one with a spire, "is the one I don't go to."

The Beach Hat

One day Aunty Megan decided to take her grandson Gareth, Ianto's son, to the beach at Borth. She arrived at the house in her grey Morris Minor and Ianto helped her to load up with a deck chair, shrimping net, bucket and spade, Gareth's bathing costume and – nearly forgot – his beach hat. He was quite fair and they didn't want him sunburnt!

They arrived at the beach – a long stretch of sand – and it was a lovely sunny day. Aunty Megan set Gareth down with his bucket and spade and started to struggle with the deck chair. Eventually she got it up and was settling down with the *Western Mail* and her knitting when she remembered she must see to his hat. So she plonked it on his head and returned to the chair.

As she sat there in the heat, knitting and reading, she began to doze off. Gradually, unnoticed by her, the tide crept closer and closer. Then there came a wave which was larger than the others – almost a freak wave. The sound of it so close by woke her up, only to see her precious grandson being dragged out to sea. In no time he was out of sight

In her distress, Megan cried out to Almighty God. She was a regular chapel goer – Corrugated Baptist.

"God," she cried, "what have you done?

How can I go back to my son and his wife and break this to them? How could I face them? Please restore my grandson to me. Take my life if you will. I am old but he has his whole life before him.

And then – literally out of the blue – came

a streak of lightning and an enormous clap of thunder. Another freak wave crashed onto the beach depositing little Gareth at his grandmother's feet. Her relief was indescribable. She grabbed him in her arms and looked down on his dripping head. Then she turned her eyes heavenward to address her maker once more.

"But God *bach*," she cried, "where's his hat?"

Death Notice

Dai went into the offices of the *Cambrian News* in Aberystwyth.

"How much does it cost to put in a death notice?" he asked the clerk.

"A pound a word," she replied.

"OK, put this: 'Thomas Evans is dead.'"

"Fine sir, that will be eight pounds."

"But you said a pound a word!"

"Oh yes, sir, but it's a minimum charge of eight pounds."

Dai thought for a bit.

"OK," he said, "put this: "Thomas Evans is dead – we also sell scaffolding."

Dai and Ianto

Dai and Ianto had been to see Wales play England at Twickenham and were returning home. It was a wet and windy January night. They had just passed the sign for the Leigh Delamere services on the M4 when Dai noticed that the fuel indicator was flashing empty. The next services were 35 miles further on, so they decided to turn off and look for a petrol station. Predictably enough they did not find one before the car spluttered to a halt in a lay-by off a narrow country lane.

It was pouring down and Dai's soft-top convertible started leaking badly. So they decided to look for shelter and set off down the lane. After about half a mile they spotted a farmhouse with a light in an upper window across several ploughed fields. So off they trudged – soon up to their ankles in mud.

They arrived at the house and knocked at the door several times. Eventually the lighted upper window opened and a face appeared – a fiftyish, round-faced country woman. They explained the situation and asked for shelter for the night. But she was very reluctant to let them in.

"I have to think of my reputation," she explained. (Well, this was 1959.) "I am a maiden lady and have lived alone here since my parents died… and I don't know you from Adam. You might be anybody."

But Dai and Ianto pleaded with her and eventually she relented. She allowed them to come in but on the strict understanding that they were to have no contact with her. She would remain on the first floor and they were strictly confined to the ground floor.

So the night passed and the following morning Dai and Ianto motored on home.

Nine months later, Dai went round to Ianto's house for a word.

"Ianto," he said, "you remember going to Twickenham?"

"Yes, Dai."

"You remember the car breaking down?"

"Yes, Dai."

"You remember we stayed at that farmhouse?"

"Yes, Dai."

"You remember we were supposed to stay on the ground floor?"

"Well... yes, Dai."

Ianto was beginning to look a little shamefaced.

"You didn't, did you, Ianto?"

"No, Dai."

"No, Ianto, you didn't. You went upstairs, didn't you... and you... well, you know."

"Well, actually, yes, Dai."

"And what's more, Ianto, you gave her my name."

"Well… er… um… sorry, Dai… but yes, I did."

"Well, thank you very much, Ianto. She's just died and left me the farm."

Santa in Sainsbury's

Here's a riddle for you:

The scene is a supermarket. There are three characters present: a rich Cardiganshire solicitor, a poor Cardiganshire solicitor and Santa Claus. There is a ten-pound note on the floor and one of them picks it up and pockets it.

The question is: which one?

The answer is the rich Cardiganshire solicitor because the other two characters are figments of your imagination.

The Hula Hula Girl

When I was growing up in Aberystwyth my best friend was called Anthony. His father had been in the navy in the war and had died when his ship was torpedoed in one of the Russian convoys. So his mother brought him up single handed – waiting for the Orange helpline.

When he left school he decided that he wanted to go to sea. As you can imagine, his mother was very much against it. But he was not to be dissuaded and joined the Royal Navy.

It was a tearful farewell on the railway platform and as they were saying goodbye his mother urged him to be sure and write regularly – indeed, she had already slipped a pack of self-addressed postcards in his case.

Anthony was not a very good correspondent and she did not hear from him for quite a long time. But eventually a postcard came:

"Dear Mam, I can't say where I am because of security, but yesterday I went ashore and shot a polar bear."

Another month's wait and then another postcard:

"Dear Mam, can't say where I am because of security, but yesterday I went ashore and danced with a Hula Hula girl."

Another month and then another postcard:

"Dear Mam, can't say where I am because of security, but I have been to see the ship's doctor. He says I would have done better to have danced with the polar bear – and shot the Hula Hula girl."

Little Dai in Oxford

This joke concerns Little Dai from the Valleys, who won the lottery. He didn't rush out, as someone from the Valleys normally would, and buy the biggest house in Fochrhiw and an American car with fins – mainly because it actually wasn't a very big win. In fact it was only enough for a Bargain Break Weekend then on special offer from Trust House Forte, which Blodwen had seen advertised in the South Wales Echo. So that's what Dai and Blodwen decided to do.

Where to go? That was no problem. Blodwen's favourite programme on television was *Inspector Morse*. So Oxford it had to be.

On the appointed day they arrived at Oxford and checked in to their hotel – then straight out to look at the sights. Blodwen was really enjoying herself, seeing all the locations which had featured on *Morse*. But there was one she was particularly keen to see. In the latest episode the body had been found in the Bodleian Library so that's where she wanted to go next.

"Dai," she said, "find out where the library's to."

It so happened that coming up the High at that moment, pushing his bicycle, was a tall figure wearing corduroy trousers, a tweed jacket with leather elbow patches and half-moon spectacles – the uniform of a Fellow of All Souls.

Dai went up to him and enquired: "Oi, butt, where's the library to?"

The bicyclist stopped, pulled himself up to his full six foot two height and looked down his long nose on all five foot five of Little Dai.

"I would have thought that even in the Valleys of Wales, from where, by your accent, I judge you to hail, it would have been axiomatic that it was inadmissible to end a sentence with a preposition," he stated.

Dai thought for a couple of seconds and replied: "OK, where's the library to, arsehole?"

Lower Corris

Iolo lived in Corris – Lower Corris, actually. One day he decided to emigrate. (Well, wouldn't you? If you can't answer that, you are obviously not familiar with Corris.) But where to go? He was not particularly well educated and was not very good at geography. So he decided to wait till the twice-monthly library bus came round the following Tuesday.

When the bus arrived, he went and borrowed the atlas. He opened it at random and stuck a pin in which landed on Timbuktu. So that was it.

Next morning he gathered his meagre possessions and set off to the General Stores. Mrs Williams, General Stores, had the agency in Corris for the Crossville Bus Company and sold the tickets.

"Morning, Iolo," said Mrs Williams, "what can we do for you?"

"Morning, Mrs Williams. I'd like a ticket to Timbuktu."

"Never heard of it, to be honest. But I'll look it up in my book. No, can't see it. Tell you what, I'll give you a ticket to Aberystwyth and you can ask from there."

So Iolo went to Aberystwyth and approached the ticket office in the railway station. Again the clerk was unable to locate Timbuktu and offered a ticket to Paddington.

Again no luck and an offer of a ticket to Heathrow.

At Heathrow he was more lucky. At least they had heard of it and sold him a ticket to Khartoum. From there, Iolo travelled by train at first and then by

mule until he eventually made it to Timbuktu.

There Iolo set up a dairy business, as you do, and prospered. But after five years he was homesick and decided to return to Wales. So he gathered up his possessions – which were more substantial by now – and went to the travel office in Timbuktu.

"I'd like a ticket to Corris."

The clerk looked at him quizzically over his spectacles and asked, "Corris, sir? Upper or Lower?"

Weights and Measures

My cousin Idris had a dairy business in London. He was forever getting into trouble with the Weights and Measures Department of the London County Council about the quality of his milk.

When this happened he would always consult my other cousin, Rhodri, who is a solicitor. Rhodri was not particularly keen to be involved – partly because he knew he would never get his fee and partly because Idris would insist on pleading not guilty, however strong the evidence.

On one occasion I remember them arguing at a family get-together.

"Look, Idris," Rhodri was saying, "it's no use going on about all the evidence being circumstantial. They did, after all, find a trout in the milk."

The Chemist's Shop

My brother David was a doctor in Tregaron. Like many doctors, his writing was almost totally illegible.

One of his patients, Evan Jones, had contacted malaria during the Malayan Emergency and David had prescribed quinine. One day the patient's wife called in to the surgery to pick up the repeat prescription and took it to the local chemists. I remember the shop well. It was pleasantly old fashioned with large blue and white jars and drawers inscribed with abbreviated Latin names for drugs. Anyway, the chemist duly gave her the package and put the money in the old-fashioned till he had and she left to do the rest of her shopping. As she walked down the street, she heard the sound of someone running and turned to see the chemist rushing up to her.

"Oh, Mrs Jones," he said, panting, "is it quinine Evan has?"

"Yes, indeed."

"Thank God I caught you in time. I've given you strychnine."

Mrs Jones looked at him bemused. "Strychnine, quinine... what's the difference?

"Well," said the chemist, "ninepence."

29

Looking at the Chickens

A friend of mine is a solicitor in Cardigan. His is a long-established family practice and he often finds himself attending his clients' weddings, funerals, etc. On one occasion he was invited to the wedding of the daughter of one client who was marrying, in fact, the son of another client. Both were local farming families. A good time was, as they say, had all round.

It seemed an entirely suitable match and my friend was very surprised, two weeks later, to find the bride in his office, in tears, asking for his help in getting a divorce. He tried to calm her down.

"Come on now," he said. "It's just a tiff, I'm sure. We'll soon have you together again." And so on.

But no amount of cajoling would budge her. She wanted a divorce.

So what was the trouble?

"Excessive sexual demands," she said.

"Oh, come, come," said my friend, soothingly. "You've only been married for five minutes. Sometimes these things take a bit of time to settle. You'll sort it out."

But she was insistent; she wanted a divorce.

"I see," he said. "I suppose you had better tell me a bit more about it – give me some examples."

"Well, yesterday I was bending over looking at the chickens and he took me from behind."

So my friend got back into soothing mode: "Mmmm… a bit rough maybe… But he loves you and he really fancies you. He will calm down in time."

Then he suddenly had a thought. He knew the farm where they lived very well.

"Chickens?" he said. "You haven't got any chickens."

"No," she said, "this was in Sainsbury's."

The Burglary

In about 1969, I think, there was quite a stir in the Tregaron area when a local farmhouse was burgled and £3,000 in cash was stolen from inside a mattress. Next Monday in Aberystwyth – market day – the town was full of Cardiganshire farmers with a new-found faith in the banking system.

I remember hearing of one who went into Lloyds Bank, Terrace Road, and produced from under his long mac a rusty old bucket, full to the brim with banknotes. He placed it on the counter, saying to the teller: "Count it." (Cardiganshire farmers don't even waste words.)

There were lots of notes and the counting took some time, but eventually it was over and the teller announced the result: £2,000. The farmer looked puzzled and tersely ordered a recount. The recount brought the same result.

A look of annoyance crossed the farmer's face. "Damn," he said, "wrong bucket."

Idris and Heulwen

Idris had had a very successful milk business in London and when he sold out to Express Dairies he had quite a tidy fortune. And he knew how to look after it. It wasn't so much that he was mean, but even in his retirement he loved a deal and always had to have an angle on everything. All this sometimes got on Heulwen's nerves. With a big house in the country, she fancied herself as a bit of a lady now and above wheeling and dealing. But they got along fine and it came as a great blow to Idris when the doctor told them that Heulwen was fatally ill. Idris was genuinely fond of her – and she had worked hard in the business and been a considerable factor in its success.

As the end neared, he took on much of the nursing himself. He wasn't much of a one for expressing his emotions but he did get round to telling her how much he felt for her.

"You've been a wonderful wife to me, Heulwen. Couldn't have asked for better. Now is there anything I can do for you to comfort you in your final hours?"

She thought for a bit and replied thoughtfully: "Actually there is. I want you to buy me something."

"Of course, dearest, you can have anything you

want. What would you like?"

"Well, Idris, I don't mind what it is. But I want you to buy it… retail."

The Travelling Players

In 1964, Aberystwyth received a visit from a travelling production of *Richard III*. It was a bit of a shoestring affair playing at various makeshift venues throughout Wales, but it had somehow managed to secure the services of Wilfred Lawson who was a well-known film and stage actor – even if he was, at that particular stage of his career, a little down on his luck.

The venue was the hastily prepared Parish Hall. The play was to be on for a week, with a matinee performance on Wednesday. Come Wednesday, three-quarters of an hour before the performance, there was no sign of Lawson or one of the other actors. Lawson was a notorious drinker and the producer took no time at all in guessing that the actors had forgotten about the matinee and would be happily ensconced in one of Aber's 36 pubs.

So the assistant stage manager was dispatched to find them. Luckily he soon did and the by-now roaring drunk pair were rushed back to the Parish Hall in time for a quick change and a dash of make-up before the play started.

Of the pair, the first to appear was Lawson. He stumbled on and soon his slurred words were echoing round the nearly empty hall. His condition was all too obvious and one of the members of audience shouted out: "You're drunk."

Lawson paused for a moment, a bit taken aback. Then he approached the front of the stage and addressed the audience directly: "You think I'm drunk? Wait till you see the Duke of Buckingham!"

The Roll of Andrex

The scene is the General Stores in Tregaron.

Enter a small boy carrying a double roll of toilet paper.

"Mam says can you swap this for a packet of Woodbines? The visitors didn't come."

Sea Sickness

How do you cure a Cardi of sea sickness?

Get him to clench a five-pound note between his teeth.

Committeemanship

Two Welshmen on a desert island.

What's the first thing they do?

Form a committee.

The Welsh News

Breaking news:

We are getting reports of a serious accident in Tregaron.

Two taxis have collided.

Twenty-eight people injured.

The Sugar Lump

One of the disadvantages of being a Welsh solicitor is that all your relatives in West Wales expect your advice for free. And the further west you go the worse they are.

My cousin Ceri from Cardigan had won the lottery and wanted my advice on investment, tax and other matters. Despite his win, I did not really expect anything in the way of a fee from him. He always ate his meals from a drawer in the kitchen table so that if visitors called he could shut the drawer as soon as he heard them knock.

One of his worries was what to do about the begging letters. But he had thought about it for a bit and decided to go on sending them.

Anyway, as I was going down that way to see him, I decided to do a couple of other duty calls on the way.

First stop was Bridgend to see Auntie Mair. She gave me a cup of tea. I took one sip and asked for a spot more sugar since I have a very sweet tooth. Fair play to the old girl, after the slightest of pauses and the most fleeting of frowns, she pushed the sugar bowl in my direction.

Then it was Carmarthen to see Auntie Phoebe. Again a cup of tea. Again the request for more sugar. But this time no question of pushing the bowl in my direction. Just a reluctant arm stretching over to take a sugar cube from the bowl and dropping it in my cup.

And so eventually to Cardigan. Cup of tea. A spot more sugar, please. But this time no sugar bowl, not even a solitary lump – just Cousin Ceri asking intently: "Are you sure you've stirred?"

Y Tŷ Bach

A professional colleague of mine had to conduct a court case in Welsh. He was a fluent native speaker but his education and professional experience had been largely in English while his Welsh remained of the homely variety.

He discovered that in the case, he would have occasion to refer to lavatory paper. He knew an informal Welsh word for it but could not think of one that would be appropriate for court use, so he consulted his father-in-law.

"Well, I don't know really," he replied. "We just called it the *Western Mail*."

Bats in the Belfry

The Vicar of Saint Mary's in Cardigan was attending the Synod of the Church in Wales in Lampeter. In the coffee break he bumped into the Vicar of Blaenporth and the Vicar of Ciliau Aeron and started chatting. As they all had rural parishes they found they had many problems in common. In particular they found that they had each had to deal with infestations of bats in their churches.

The Vicar of Blaenporth explained how he had tried to deal with the problem. He had asked a parishioner who had a shotgun to shoot the creatures. This had worked in that he got rid of the bats, but at the cost of considerable damage to the fabric of the church building.

The Vicar of Ciliau Aeron said that he had tried a more humane way. He had laid a net in the nave and baited it. When the bats swarmed on the bait he had caught them in the net. After this he was reluctant to kill them – they were, after all, God's creatures – so he had taken them to a local wood and released them. The trouble was that bats have a homing instinct and within half an hour they were all back in the church.

The Vicar of Cardigan then explained his solution. He had done the same business with the net and the bait and managed to catch all the bats.

But what he did then was to baptise the bats and arrange for the bishop to confirm them – he had even married some of them.

"And, do you know," he said, "not one of the blighters has been near the place since."

The Town Clock

As part of the Millennium celebrations, Aberystwyth built a new town clock to replace the one that had been demolished many years earlier. This story relates back to the time of the old clock.

In those days there had been a public lavatory at the site of the clock. The walls of this lavatory were covered with the usual graffiti to which some wit had added the inscription:

"The views expressed on these walls are not necessarily the views of the Aberystwyth Urban District Council."

Llandrindod Wells

I was very surprised when my aunt told me she was intending to retire to Llandrindod Wells.

"But Auntie Megan," I said, "why there? We don't have any family or any connections in that part of Wales."

"Well, Huw *bach*," she said, "what I feel is that I am now coming to the evening of my life, and in Llandrindod, the transition from life to death is… hardly perceptible."

Ianto Goes Courting

Ianto decided it was time he was wed. Well, his father and mother were getting on and he would soon need help around the farm. Trouble was, living in the back of beyond, he did not have much of a chance to meet girls. But he did go to chapel every Sunday so he decided to look around there. When he saw a girl he fancied, he'd invite her back to Sunday tea. But the problem was his mother did not like any of them.

With the first one it was the way she dressed.

With the second it was the way she talked.

With the third it was the way she did her hair.

But on the fourth try Ianto thought he had it cracked. The thing with this one was, she was exactly like his mother – same dress sense, same way of talking, same hairstyle.

But it was no good – his father couldn't stand her.

The Ten Commandments

My Uncle Idwal was born in a village in the north of Cardiganshire in about, I would say, 1918. His parents were poor but fiercely ambitious for their children and very keen on education. Idwal was a clever lad and his hard work in the primary school was rewarded with a scholarship to the grammar school in Aberystwyth. He worked hard there as well and won an open scholarship to New College, Oxford. At Oxford he kept his head down — he could not afford the social whirl anyway — and got a good first.

At this stage the world would normally have been his oyster. He could have gone anywhere and done anything. But for his generation, of course, it was the war. He was commissioned in a Tank Regiment. He had a good war and at end of it, again, his prospects were unlimited. But the experience of war had changed him; he had discovered within himself a vocation to the Christian Ministry. So turning aside from the prospects of glittering prizes, he qualified as a Baptist Minister and returned to the small chapel in which his family had worshipped.

After he had been there for about a year, something happened which deeply shocked him. He went to his shed one day to get his bicycle and there it was — gone. And remember this is not the inner city in the 21st century, this was rural Cardiganshire in the 1950s; a nicked bike was a crime wave.

He thought about it for some time and eventually decided what he would do. Next Sunday he would go, as they say, back to basics — and take his flock through the Ten Commandments. And he would keep an eye out when he came to the one about theft, to see if there were any shifty reactions.

So there they all were, his faithful flock, hanging on to his every word. Off he went:

Thou shalt have no other gods before me.

Thou shalt not make unto thee any graven image.

(You can tell I had a good Christian education – I had the catechism beaten into me.)

Anyway, when he came to the one about adultery, he remembered where he had left his bike.

Cardiganshire DIY

A friend calls at Dai's house and finds him stripping wallpaper.

"Hello, Dai. Decorating?"

"No," says Dai. "Moving."

The Window Cleaner

A Cardiganshire window cleaner had an accident at work. He was up his ladder when he took a rag out of his pocket and accidentally dislodged a fifty-pence piece. He went down to get it and it caught him in the eye.

A Round of Golf

Late on in his life, Uncle Idwal took up golf – partly for something to occupy him when he retired from the Church. And, boy, did he get the bug! He played as often as he could and always kept his clubs in the boot of his ancient grey Morris Minor wherever he went.

In summer he often used to help out his clerical colleagues by standing in for them when they took their holidays. So one summer weekend found him returning home from a church in North Wales where he had held the morning service. As he was travelling through Harlech he decided, on an impulse, to turn off and have a look at the golf course. No possibility of him actually playing, of course – he was a strict observer of the Sabbath. But there was no harm in looking.

He had heard a lot about the golf course – one of the very best in Wales – and had always wanted to play there. It lived up to all his expectations – it was glorious. And it was a glorious day. And… well, he was tempted. He looked around. There were not many people about. He was quite a way from home. Nobody would know. So he sidled round to the pro's shop and paid the green fee.

So there he was – on the first tee. A couple of practice shots. Now for his first drive. Fantastic.

Straight down the middle. A country mile.

Now at exactly this moment, who happened to be passing, also coincidentally, in a battered grey Morris Minor, but Father Padraig Murphy, the local catholic priest? Glancing at the course as he drove by, he saw Uncle Idwal striding down the first fairway after his ball. His reaction was one of shock and, to be frank, a degree of malicious enjoyment.

Parking his car and getting out, he addressed our Creator: "Well! Have you seen t'at?"

"Yes, actually, I had noticed," replied the Almighty somewhat tetchily. "I am omniscient and omnipresent, you know."

"Never mind all that," said Father Murphy, "what are you going to do about it?"

"Well, as a matter of fact, I have got a plan."

"Well, what is it?"

"Ahaa… you'll just have to wait and see, won't you?"

So Father Murphy took a seat on a bench overlooking the course and waited expectantly. He saw Uncle Idwal take his approach shot to the first green and he creamed it – three feet from the pin – then he holed the putt for a birdie.

A bit disappointing for the priest, but no doubt God was just building Idwal up for the fall. What would it be? Would his game collapse? That would hardly suffice. Maybe a thunderbolt? But no, the game continued in the same way and Idwal played the round every golfer dreams of. What was God up to?

Eventually Idwal finished his round. At one of the best and most difficult courses in the country, he had scored ten under his handicap. He'd never done anything like it before.

Father Murphy turned to the Almighty in disgust and said, "What on earth (or indeed heaven) are you doing?"

"Think about it, my son," came the reply. "Who can he tell?"

Le Bordel

Dai is in Paris for the rugby match. At the end of the evening he finds himself in a very smart brothel. He asks the Madam for a ham sandwich and the ugliest woman she can find.

"But, Monsieur," she protests, "this is the finest brothel in Paris. You can have the finest French cuisine and choose from a selection of the most beautiful women imaginable."

"But I'm not hungry and I'm not horny," he replied. "I'm homesick."

The Bunch of Grapes

Small boy visiting neighbour's house with his mother:

"*Duw*, there's posh – grapes and nobody ill."

Sex on a Sunday

They were a young couple very much in love. But they were strictly brought-up chapel people and only wanted to do what was right. In particular they were concerned about whether it was right to make love on the Sabbath.

They decided to ask for advice from their minister. He wasn't quite sure either, so he took further advice from the National Council of the Presbyterian Church in Wales. After much deliberation he was able to give them the answer to their question.

"It's alright," he told them, "as long as you don't enjoy it."

Other Jokes

Did you know that 74 per cent of households in Tregaron take the *Cambrian News*?

The other 26 per cent pay for it.

★ ★ ★

What did he die of then?

Oooooooooh… nothing serious.

The departed was lying in an open coffin as the neighbours came round to offer their respects.

"He really looks peaceful and content," said one.

"Yes," said the widow, "that week in Porthcawl did him the world of good."

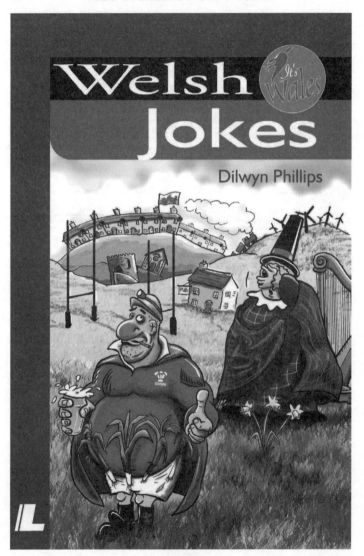

£3.95

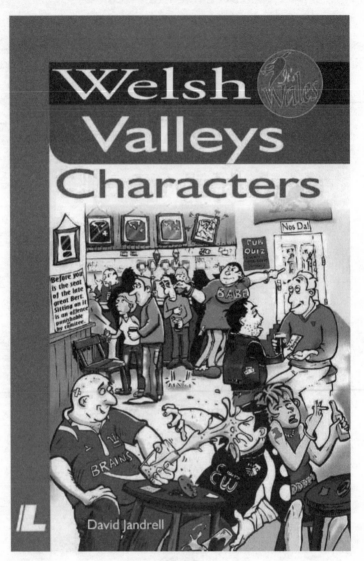

Welsh Valleys Characters

David Jandrell

Nos Da!

PUB QUIZ

Before you is the seat of the late great Bert. Sitting on it is an offence punishable by comitee.

BABE

BRAINS

£3.95

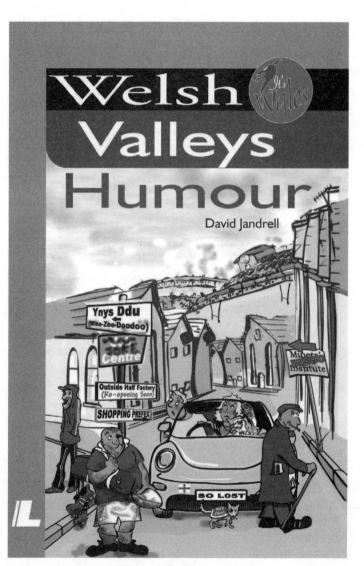

£3.95

More
Welsh Jokes

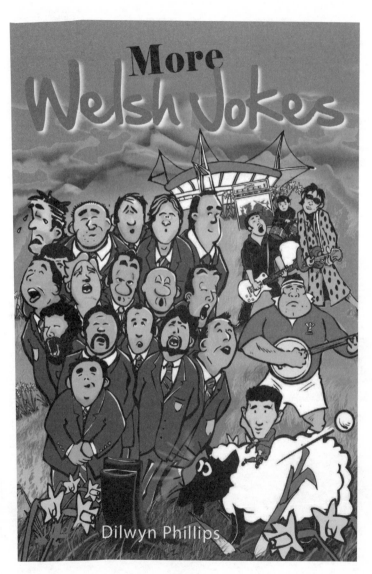

Dilwyn Phillips

£3.95

The Half-Tidy Book of Welsh Jokes is just one of a whole range of publications from Y Lolfa. For a full list of books currently in print, send now for your free copy of our new full-colour catalogue. Or simply surf into our website

www.ylolfa.com

for secure on-line ordering.

TALYBONT CEREDIGION CYMRU SY24 5HE
e-mail ylolfa@ylolfa.com
website www.ylolfa.com
phone (01970) 832 304
fax 832 782